Published by Sourcebooks eXplore, an imprint of Sourcebooks Kids

P.O. Box 4410, Naperville, Illinois 60567-4410

(630) 961-3900

sourcebookskids.com

First published as *Red Kangaroo's Thousands Physics Whys: Fly Fly to the Sky: the Science of Flying* in 2018 in China by China Children's Press and Publication Group. All rights reserved.

Library of Congress Cataloging-in-Publication Data is on file with the publisher.

Source of Production: PrintPlus, Shenzhen, Guangdong Province, China

Date of Production: February 2020

Run Number: 5017053

Printed and bound in China.

PP 10 9 8 7 6 5 4 3 2 1

Let's Fly a Plane!

Launching into the Science of Flight with Aerospace Engineering

sourcebooks
eXplore

**#1 Bestselling
Science Author for Kids
Chris Ferrie**

Red Kangaroo sees an airplane in the sky. She wants to fly too! But when she jumps, Red Kangaroo comes down with a thump.

"How can something so big stay in the sky when I cannot?" she wonders. "Dr. Chris will know!"

Red Kangaroo finds Dr. Chris in his lab. "Can you tell me how planes fly?" she asks him.

"Of course," Dr. Chris says. "You just need to know some aerospace engineering!"

"Please teach me!" Red Kangaroo replies.

"I want to jump and fly high in the sky!"

"Anything can fly with a little help from four forces. They are lift, thrust, drag, and weight," Dr. Chris says. "Have you heard of any of them before?"

Lift

Drag

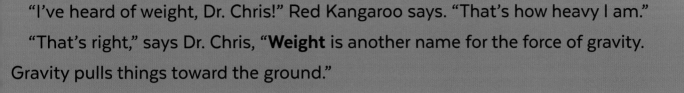

"I've heard of weight, Dr. Chris!" Red Kangaroo says. "That's how heavy I am."

"That's right," says Dr. Chris, "**Weight** is another name for the force of gravity. Gravity pulls things toward the ground."

Weight

"Is gravity the force that keeps me from jumping super high?" Red Kangaroo asks.

"Yes," Dr. Chris replies. "If you were on the Moon, you would be much lighter and would be able to stay up in the air longer when you jump. That's because the Moon has less gravity than Earth."

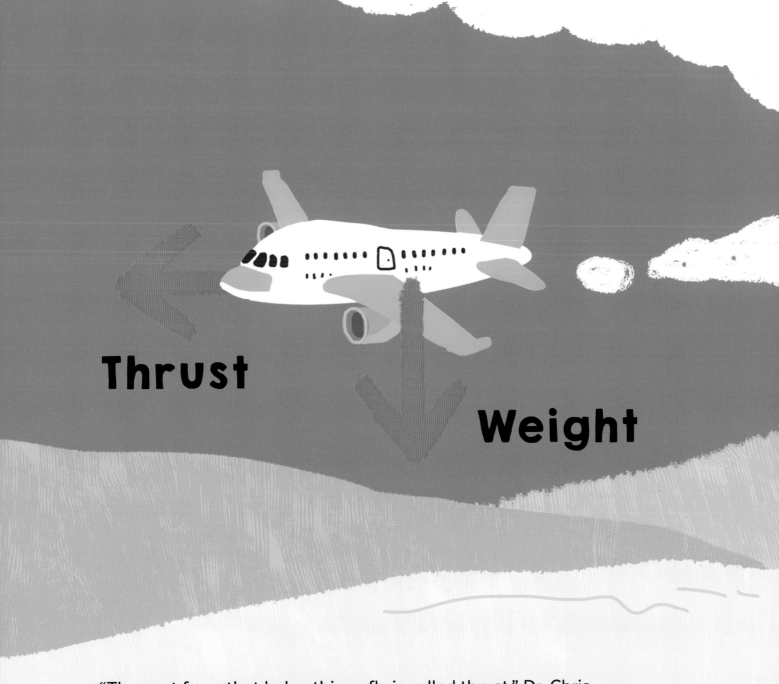

Thrust

Weight

"The next force that helps things fly is called thrust," Dr. Chris continues. "**Thrust** makes objects zoom forward. Engines are used to create this force for vehicles like planes, cars, and trains."

"Thrust obeys an important rule called Newton's Third Law of Motion. This rule says that for every force, there is an equal force in the opposite direction. An engine pushes air out with fiery force. This air going out pushes the plane forward!"

"So there's a force pulling the plane down and a force pushing it forward. Is there a force pointing backward too?" asks Red Kangaroo.

"Yes! **Drag** is the name of the force that tries to stop motion," Dr. Chris replies. "It is the force of friction. Can you guess what's causing the friction?"

Dr. Chris

"I know, I know!" says Red Kangaroo. "It must be because the plane is moving against the air!"

"Exactly! Friction is very important," Dr. Chris says. "Without it, things wouldn't be able to stop moving."

"Like that time I tried to run across a frozen pond," says Red Kangaroo. "I couldn't stop until I hit the ground!"

"I think I know the last force, Dr. Chris," Red Kangaroo says. "The last force must be lift. There is only one arrow missing and it goes up!"

Lift

Thrust

Drag

Weight

"That's right. Good job, Red Kangaroo! All four forces balance each other so that the plane keeps a steady motion in the sky."

Cross-section of a plane wing

"To have lift, you need a very special shape. A plane's wings provide the perfect shape to produce the right lift. If we look at the wing from its side, it looks like this."

"Because of this unique shape, air travels over the wing in a pattern that is different from the air that flows under the wing. The difference in airflow is what causes **lift**."

"I understand now, Dr. Chris!"
says Red Kangaroo.

"Lift, thrust, drag, and weight. I have mastered the four forces of flight!" says Red Kangaroo. "So now can I fly?"

"You have them mastered, but I think we will still need some help from engineers," Dr. Chris replies.

"This is more like it!" shouts Red Kangaroo.

"Now we're flying!"

Glossary

Aerospace Engineering
The study of vehicles that move through the air.

Airflow
The way air moves around an object.

Drag
A force that works to stop something from moving through the air.

Force
Any push or pull on an object.

Friction
A force that works to stop something from moving across a surface.

Gravity
A force that pulls two objects to each other. Earth's gravity is what makes things fall and what keeps you on the ground.

Lift
A force on something moving through air and changing the airflow.

Newton's Third Law of Motion

For every force there is an equally strong force acting in the opposite direction.

Thrust

A force that pushes something to move in a specific direction. Engines produce thrust for vehicles like planes.

Weight

The force of gravity on an object. The direction of this force always pulls down.

Show What You Know

1. Name the four forces that help a plane fly.

2. A plane's engine causes thrust and pushes the plane forward. Describe what causes the force of lift on a plane.

3. One of the four forces that help airplanes fly disappears after a paper airplane leaves your hand. Can you identify which one?

4. Name the one force that is always acting on you.

5. Explain why you weigh less on the Moon. (Need a hint? Go back and read pages 10-11.)

Answers on last page.

Test It Out

What a drag!

Create three (or more!) paper airplanes. Try to make them so they are all the same size and style. (If you need help, ask an adult to help you look for designs online. There are many different styles to choose from, but Dr. Chris suggests "the dart.")

Use scissors to make two small cuts in the back end of the wing. Then fold up the cut part to create flaps. Try creating different-sized flaps for each paper airplane.

Predict how far each plane will fly. Will a bigger flap cause more drag than a smaller flap?

Let your airplanes fly! Make sure to throw all of them in the same way and from the same place.

Measure how far each plane flew and record your answers. Which flaps created more drag to stop the planes? Were your predictions correct?

Try the experiment again with the flaps turned down. Do you get the same results?

If you want to test out lift, create paper airplanes that have different-size wings. Then let them fly. The wings with better airflow will fly further.

Flying without lift?

Gather the following supplies: a sheet of notebook or computer paper, tape, and a drinking straw.

Cut the sheet of paper so that it is as long as the straw and is wide enough to wrap around the straw.

Wrap the cut-out piece of paper around the straw and tape it closed. (You should have a tube of paper the same shape as the straw now.)

Fold one end of your paper tube closed and tape it shut. Make sure you're not bending or taping the straw when you do this. You should have a small bit of the straw sticking out on the other end.

You now have a mini rocket! Blow into the straw at the end that's not taped and watch your rocket zoom! What force did your breath give the rocket to make it fly?

Ready your rocket for flight again, but this time add wings to it by taping triangular pieces of paper to the sides. Make a prediction about whether this will change how high or how far your rocket will go.

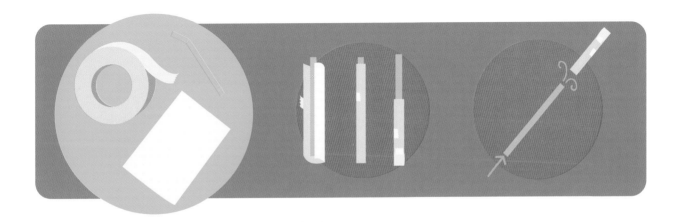

What to expect when you Test It Out

What a drag!

The paper airplanes with smaller flaps should create less drag than the airplanes with bigger flaps. The bigger flaps experience more friction from the air which stops the plane from flying.

Flying without lift?

You give the rocket thrust with your breath. Adding wings to your plane might slow it down because the wings will create more drag, but the wings will not make your rocket fly higher. Thrust is the only thing that can help a rocket overcome gravity.

Show What You Know answers

1. Lift, thrust, drag, and weight.

2. Air moving around the wings.

3. Thrust.

4. Weight (caused by gravity).

5. The Moon has less mass and so there is less gravity.